Heart

of the

White Dove

Journeys to the Light

Pam Sears

ISBN: 978-1981468355

First Printing: December, 2017

Published by 102nd Place LLC
Scottsdale, AZ 85266

Dedication

To my two sons Arthur and Douglas

and

To all the dreamers and adventurers who
live life to the fullest
and never give up.

Table of Contents

My Story

50

So now you are 50
What have you to say?
You look so forward
To a brand new day!

Don't look to the past
Face forward and see
The whole and complete person
You so yearned to be!

You are finally there
Please stand proud and tall
And know to get up
Whenever you fall.

The lessons aren't over
But now you can see
To face them head on
Will set your heart free!

The struggles, the strife,
And at times much pain
Only made you much stronger
Such wisdom you gained!

What has all come before
Please never forget
But look at you now
No need for regret.

Take what you have learned
Put it wisely to use
And spread it with love
And reject all abuse!

For what you now know
Take this wisdom with care
Help all who are seeking
And this healing, please share!

For now you are whole
Your being complete
Time to reach out to others
Without need to compete!

Keep open the heart
Set ego aside
Continue to love
With arms open wide!

Live life with pure joy
Start each day with a smile
Remember to love you
And to sit for a while.

Each day is adventure
Each day you are free
So take a few risks
But keep your integrity!

Like a Dove in a cage
You've opened the door
And set that bird free
So now watch her soar!!!

January 2004

Balance

Among the mess
The chaos and debris
I'm shown a way
To set it all free

Two hawks on the branch
Two turtles on the ground
One hawk chooses to eat
One on branch looks down

Choices are placed
Decisions are there
Focus my intent
But choosing beware

By making the choice
Does balance then come?
Am I on the same path?
Or have lessons begun?

In order to achieve
The balance here
I must walk the path
Letting go of the fear

Trust what is inside
The soul truly knows
The balance is there
And the fire glows

Seek out the wheel
Of balance and pride
Only then can I share
The truth deep inside

Balance within
Is balance without
A way is shown
So I take this route

At the end of the road
I shall surely see
I made the right choice
Found deep inside me

June 2005

Sweet Surrender

Silky flow
As a river stream
Water so clear
A summer's glow

The water soothes
Down to the soul
What lies up ahead
There are no clues

It feels like the sky
Brings itself close to me
I can touch the clouds
With no need to ask why

Swirling to and fro
Floating face up
I'm able to see
God's awesome glow

Surrender to life
Tis sweet it is
Makes it flow as a river
With much less strife

This river of Love
Is for all to feel
Once surrender is given
It fits like a glove

Surrender you see
Takes hardly a thought
Just give it a try
At once you are free

It's not in our control
Where the river takes us
So enjoy the journey
It brings peace to the soul

July 2006

Maiden, Mother, Crone

In a young woman's life, her teen and young adulthood time, she is considered the maiden, young and carefree and beginning her life. Enjoying all that life gives and learning how to become a woman into her own right.

Then later, as she becomes Mother, her second path of Life begins; a new journey of self-sacrifice and giving birth not only to children, but many other things. Mothers are the true nurturers and healers, and so very giving and full of Love for her off-spring, even at the risk of heartache, for children can be very trying at times. Her life is on hold for the most part as she commits herself to raising a family.

But alas, the third and final path of her journey comes and this is a time of renewal and a brand new dance, some call it the change of Life, Menopause . . . but the Native Americans and other cultures call it Crone hood: a very revered and respected title. When a woman turns 52, she then becomes a Crone, an elder, a wise woman, even teacher. She has raised her children, taught them the best she could and now has a new purpose unfolding. Her last journey of her earth walk, her new dance of life begins; she has earned this revered title.

I have turned 52 this year and I am relishing the title of Crone. I enjoyed my life as Maiden and so loved my life as Mother, but now it is time for this Crone to begin a new journey and see what new purpose awaits her. I accept the Crone, the elder, however, the wise woman I am still unsure of and seek to learn more and perhaps one day I shall reach that level of wise (giggles).

My sons are almost full-grown. The youngest will be 18 next year and graduates from high school . . . becoming a man. Even now he doesn't want much to do with a "mother." He has his friends and life and seeks to break away and find his own niche. I do not take it personally. It's time for this crone to find her own way now, her own happiness, her own new purpose and where she fits in. There is no sadness, I'm ready now. My two sons are growing into men and finding their own lives and now is the time for this dove to use her wings more and journey into unknown territories.

Some friends call me whacko, and say they don't have the courage to take journeys alone up into wilderness areas as I do, and what am I thinking? I'm thinking I'm actually having the time of my life.

Perhaps I shall ask for a special crone ceremony when I go back for this year's Earth dance Ceremony in the fall. I had observed one last year and it was very powerful for the woman.

So for you women out there, next time someone tries to call you an "Old Crone" be sure and thank them, for the title is NOT a negative but quite the opposite and should be taken as a compliment!

Ok now, where did I put those dancing shoes I stored a few years ago?

Rite of Passage

She looks in the mirror
At age 52
Thinking back in her life
When she had no clue

So there's another grey hair
Well, maybe more than one
As she runs to the store
Buying hair dye by the ton

And while she's at it
She buys mustache wax
She accepts the change
Then buys her some jacks

She plays with her jacks
Remembering her youth
When boys pulled her hair
And were totally uncouth

She sits on the floor
Playing with her toys
Wax covers her lips
Eating chocolate galore

Her sons look and stare
In total shock
This can't be our mother
Turn back the clock

I'm quite okay
She says with a smile
It's my rite of passage
Let me be for awhile

They shake their heads
Hoping friends don't see
There's mom again
Hugging a tree

It's called the change
Starting a new life
Today I'm not mother,
Daughter, or wife

Today I am six
And giggling with glee
I can do what I want
Even dance naked you see

I've earned the right
And today I am free
So don't touch my candy,
My toys or my tree

I'll say what I want
I'll do as I please
I'll dance in moonlight
And do so with ease

You say I am nuts
I beg to differ my dear
It's my rite of passage
And my path is now clear

So get out of my way
Pami's coming thru
She's starting to live
Life beginning anew

Oh yes she is sane
Oh yes she is clear
This rite of passage
She honors so dear

With a smile and a shout
And a clean upper lip
She jumps into the river
Yep, to skinny dip

I honor my life
Who I truly am
Giving thanks for each day
God loves you Pam!

December 2006

Soul Cleanse

Tears down the face
Brings no disgrace
Speaks to the soul
A letting go

Floods as a river
Brings with it a shiver
Don't fight the tears
Allow the fears

Talk to the sky
When you ask why
Cradled in love
From so high above

Spirit knows it's time
It's not a crime
Be sure and just feel
Another layer thus peeled

What comes so deep
Let it go, don't keep
Send it out
With a cry and a shout

Healing does come
As a bright morning sun
With a rainbow or two
And a sky so blue

January 2007

Lizard Speaks

Dove sat there among the branches contemplating her challenges. As a dove, she is there to help others, to render aid and assistance and help in healing. She looked down upon a lizard that had stopped and looked up to her. Odd that the lizard should stay there staring so intently, yet dove did not speak to it.

The next day as dove continued to ponder her path, lizard came again and sat and stared at her. Dove wondered about this; then began to go back to her own thoughts and fears.

On the third day of her inward journey, seeking answers, the lizard came again. Lizard did as before staring intently at the dove. Finally dove said, "Lizard, why do you visit? This is the third time you have shown yourself. Could it be that you indeed have a message for me?"

Lizard smiled and found a place among the branches next to the dove. "I am glad that you have finally acknowledged me for yes I do have a message."

Dove spoke out loud in awe at the lovely long tail of the lizard and the beauty of it. Lizard began to speak in a calm and peaceful voice. "Why thank you, for this is my new and improved tail. You see Dove, we lizards are known for our resilience and strength. Our tails can be severed, but we continue on our journey still living, breathing and showing our beauty. The tail may or may not grow back, but the real truth is, we survived, we carried on and went forward on our paths. I am here to remind you that although you have this challenge, fear not, for you will survive even if your own tail gets severed. You shall carry on with strength and courage and continue to help others as you have done so before, but in a much more loving and confident way than ever before. Shine your light, for it is bright. Trust and have faith that the journey indeed goes on and all is as it should be. Remember to love yourself as well as others."

Dove had a renewed sense of faith, hope and courage and graciously thanked lizard and they both sat in silence, feeling the warmth of the sun and the love all around.

August 2014

My Story

No one ever expects the call to come, certainly not me the hospice worker, who takes care of those who are terminally ill from cancer and other illnesses. I'm a healer, I help others, and I bring comfort, and have for many years. My Hospice Life has taught me so much; from the emotional aspect, to the physical, to the spiritual.

"Pam, you have breast cancer"

What? Me? That can't be possible. No way can it be happening to me. But it was. The overwhelming shock, the feeling of having the rug pulled out from under you, and being electrocuted all at the same time. Little did I know at the time just how much my hospice work had prepared me for my temporary journey with the big "C."

Previous mammograms did not show cancer, although the lump had been there. I was informed all was well, when in reality, the cancer was growing, albeit slowly. Lobular carcinoma can only be found with a biopsy and ultrasound until it gets to be too advanced. That's what happened to me. The mass was too large. I would need a full mastectomy. In thinking back, my intuition was telling me it was something, but since I was told it was nothing, I put it all out of my mind and went on with my life. A second opinion and an ultrasound early on would have prevented a mastectomy; something for which I'm now a huge advocate. Always listen to what your body is telling you and be your own advocate!

So my temporary journey with cancer began and I had some decisions to make. I knew deep within my heart the path I was NOT going to take and that was traditional chemotherapy and radiation. As a hospice worker I have seen the after effects of both and it's not something my soul wanted! Of course I did a great deal of praying for guidance. My spiritual background gave me a huge amount of faith that whatever I chose and was guided to do, would be for my highest good! My mastectomy surgery wasn't planned for six weeks. I had already planned a trip to Hawaii on a Spiritual Retreat. I knew it would give me some important inner healing that would help me not only get through the surgery, but after as well.

I was also, through synchronicity, introduced to a Japanese biochemist in my area that had owned a cancer clinic at one time and helped a lot of stage 4 cancer patients go into complete remission. The fact that we were put together at exactly the right time, I know in my heart it was divinely inspired. This was just prior to going on my Hawaii retreat.

His protocol involved some heavy duty items and I sat and listened intently to all he had to say. There was a part of me that feared his protocol due to the fact it was very expensive, yet this was my life we were talking about. My very being screamed *Do it, this is what you have been guided to do! Here is the answer you have been praying for!*

Thank God I had my friend Martha with me for support. She said, "Pam, if this is what your heart is guiding you to, just do it and don't worry about where the money is coming from. Trust it!"

In my heart I so fully knew it was the right thing for me. The regimen included pancreatic enzymes, high doses of liquid vitamin C, coffee enemas, as well as other immune building supplements. It also involved giving up animal protein and dairy, with the exception of real butter and getting my body alkaline. I totally accepted this new way of eating and living. In fact my body responded so well that I actually began to feel 100% better. By the time I had my surgery weeks later, I have no doubt my fast healing was a direct result of taking care of myself in a healthy and natural way.

I want to share a very special message that I received while in Hawaii. Many women had said to me, "How can you even go to Hawaii knowing you have cancer?" One even said, "If it was me I couldn't wait to get that out of my body and wouldn't be able to sleep until I knew it was gone."

I wanted to acknowledge it, and listen to my body. I know it may sound odd but I thanked the cancer for waking me up to whatever it was that caused it to happen in the first place. For me I KNEW I hadn't been nurturing myself throughout all my years of helping others. Then I heard my huge message. I still recall the one day I was standing out among the lava rocks on our way to Hana in Hawaii, when I heard a very loud voice say, "You are NOT being torn apart, you are being put back right." I turned around and no one was there! But I knew it was a very special message to me coming from the universe, God, my angels, guides, whatever you wish to call it. I began to understand so much more from that point on.

The day of surgery day finally arrived. I had of course shed a few tears and grieved over what I knew I would be losing. But hey, it's just a breast right? The surgery was over, they had found some cancer in the sentinel nodes and took three more next to that to be biopsied. The doctor felt assured she got it all. I remember lying in that hospital bed and knew in my heart and soul that I would never be taking chemo or radiation. My journey would be done MY way.

I did the consults with the oncologist and radiation doctors. I just couldn't do it although they tried to instill fear, I did not take that on. My one big disappointment was while at the oncologist office (it was breast cancer awareness month) I was astounded to see so many sugary treats being handed out. I even had a woman try and shove a cookie at me saying, "You know you want this".

What?! They KNOW sugar feeds cancer. How in the hell can they offer such garbage? She was saying how the patients going through chemo need some comfort foods and they intended to sugar them up and get them out of there. That was the last time I stepped inside any oncologists' office.

I chose to continue my protocol as outlined for me which included remaining vegan, no sugar, working on my stress level, exercise, hyperthermia, and my absolute belief system that I was cancer free. I occasionally now will try wild caught salmon or halibut, but that is rare. It is now 18 months later and I remain cancer free, all tumor markers are well below normal and I feel healthier now than I have ever been in the past.

My outlook on life has also changed. Although I was mostly a positive person before, now I truly live to be alive. I take those trips I had been putting off. I'm doing those things on my bucket list and always remind myself, *life is for living*. I truly did get a second chance and I plan on taking advantage of every moment here on this Earth.

I still have some of those fears, but I am working on them and freeing those chains that bound me before. I don't tell others how to walk their own cancer journeys but if anyone wants to talk to me, I will share my own experience. The one important thing I tell everyone who contacts me is this: do your research before making any big decision. I also remind others, don't let fear make your decision for you!

Whenever anyone asks me, "do you feel you made the right decision?" I am taken back to that day where I asked myself the same question. Shortly after, a car pulled in front of me while I was driving with a license plate that read, WEBEGLAD! I smile as I recall that. It was my answer, my proof that I truly did follow my own heart. Always, always follow your heart. It will never steer you wrong.

April 2016

Cross the Bridge

Destiny calls
Hear its voice
Cross the bridge
Make a choice

Although unknown
What lies beyond
A melody lures
Such a lovely song

It calls the soul
To take the leap
Cross the bridge
An agreement to keep

Don't stop on the path
The journey's not done
One step at a time
Means you have truly won

When the Door Shuts

When the door shuts, leave it closed

You can't go back and why would you?

Perhaps it was an easier path

And the new one looks scary

But the door is shut for a reason

In spite of any fear, keep going

Going forward to your destiny

You learned what you could

From the other side of that closed door

Life isn't about easy

It's about how you walk that journey

No matter your fears

Take the step, one teeny tiny step at a time

With each step it gets easier

And you become lighter, stronger

And your light shines brighter

Leave that closed door shut

That isn't at all where you are going

But remember to thank it for the lessons

And walk forward in love, faith, and courage

October 2017

The Hidden Path

I stand before me

On a new journey

A journey of faith

Of uncertainty

Yet knowing I must walk it

I can't go back

I can't stand still

There is only movement

Not sideways, not back, but forward

Yet the path is hidden

I don't know my fate

Yet I hear the words

We have your back

Trust us

Have hope and faith

You have a story to tell

Yet you don't know the ending

And that's okay

You are the rock

You have the courage

To step into the unknown

So I take a deep breath

And begin the journey

Through the Lens

Peering through the lens

Capturing the true essence of nature

The true reality of the world

What the universe has sent to behold

The beauty, the strength the poignancy

Capturing memories but best of all

Sharing those memories with the world

With those in need of seeing that beauty

Of needing strength and love

To give them a taste of what I truly see

And feel, and hear and touch

The essence of life, real life

Real love, real beauty,

That makes me glow within

Sending out the ripple effect

Helping you glow within

Do you see and feel what I do

As I peer through the lens

Heart bursting with excitement

Passion for the adventure

And there will always be another adventure

Come join me . . . .

Muddy
Footprints

What is it that I Know?

What is it that I know?

What is it that I feel?

Sitting here in the void

Asking questions of which

No answers come

Or do they come

But blocked by ego

Not allowing ears to hear

But the soul does hear

And accepts

It is all knowing

All caring

All love

It is reality

Never illusion

So what does my soul know?

It knows it is LOVE

Receives and gives it

That it is always safe

And never abandoned

It is eternal

It sparkles

At times explodes

Into passion

As in seeing a sunrise

Or the fireworks

And the sunset

At the end of another day

Of learning and seeking

It is . . . a rainbow!

The Dragonfly and the Dove

A chance encounter
or was it fate
Brought two spirits together
On that special date

In the Divine order
Of Universal law
A moment arrived
In full glory and awe

Thus came a new path
For both to share
Joining in Love
Helping souls be aware

To brighten their spirit
And help them to shine
To remind them they are
a spark so Divine

I Do This for Me

I do this for me

It's not about you

Or them or us

Simply me

What would be the point in changing for you?

I accept you for you

Please accept me for me

The movement I feel is the soul talking

About what I agreed to do in this life

You may be part of it

You may even last a lifetime

You may last a day

Your moving on doesn't change me

Nor my moving on doesn't change you

We each walk our path

Separate and alone

Perhaps carrying memories

If pain is involved, it's a choice

But don't carry around what isn't yours

Just give it back to whomever it belongs

Lighten your backpack

It is full already of your lessons

Your life, your stories

Say goodbye with a smile

And a heartfelt thanks

And simply keep moving forward

Perhaps adding a dance to your step

We are only here for a little while

How do you wish to proceed?

Muddy Footprints

"It's time to get back to life." That's what my best friend kept saying. "It's been over a year. I know that you miss him but he wouldn't want you moping around and staying depressed."

She doesn't understand, she doesn't have a dog and isn't an animal lover. Rusty was my heart and soul, my light. He was there for me in my darkest hours and gave me unconditional love – always.

Rusty actually chose me! I had gone to a shelter right after the breakup with my ex hoping to find some healing to my hurt heart. I kept walking back and forth and this not so shy dog was doing his best to get my attention. He would run back and forth in his kennel as if he were saying, "See me, see me!" He was this scrawny looking rat terrier, not one that I would have ever picked for myself but something drew me to him. We spent over an hour communicating back and forth in his kennel and my heart had found love. For 15 years he stayed by my side.

I was once again in a breakup from a relationship and at a crossroads of whether I wanted another dog or not. My heart was still hurting from losing Rusty and then this new breakup. I was overwhelmed and couldn't decide what to do so I did nothing. My best friend Ellie was pushing me to get back at it; find another "Rusty."

"You can't replace Rusty," I told her repeatedly. I chose one Saturday afternoon to go along with Ellie and take a peek at some dogs at the shelter. My heart ached for Rusty but I kept an open mind. Perhaps my heart was still closed or I wasn't ready but none of those sweet animals resonated with me in any way. I decided to come back another day.

On our ride home it began to rain and the roads were slick and the ground got wet. I pulled into my driveway and remembered I had forgotten the mailbox. At the moment the rain had slowed to just a drizzle. I got my mail, began to walk back and noticed something on my front porch area. As I got closer I saw tiny muddy footprints leading up the walkway. I always park in my garage and rarely do I use my front door, let alone check it out. But something drew me today to do so. I have a long walkway that leads to the door. As I got closer I noticed something brown huddled by the door.

At first I wondered if it was some wild animal and called out to my friend Ellie to come see. She is much braver than I and she went ahead of me, without fear it seemed. As we got closer she yelled out, "OMG it's a dog."

Sure enough it was another terrier type dog with a cold body and warm eyes that reached directly into my heart. It was shivering and dirty and had mud all over its paws. We did not see a collar. We scooped the little guy up in our arms and drove straight to the vet to see if he was micro-chipped. No chip was found but the vet said the dog appeared to be healthy, although a tad hungry.

We took him home with me not wanting to get attached in case he had an owner. We immediately put fliers up and posted his picture on Facebook. After a week no one had claimed him. He had been getting his little spirit entwined with mine that whole week and he wouldn't leave my side. He slept with me, watched TV with me, and took walks with me. Two weeks later he and I had bonded and decided we belonged together.

Somehow in my heart I knew Rusty sent him to me. Hell, he was already AT my home, a sure fire sign it was meant to be. Some of my hurt left me and I began to heal, alongside my best new friend. All due to muddy footprints or in this case paw prints. Lol.

Chelsea

You showed in my life
To help heal my heart
I didn't want to love you
From the very start

But Soul touched soul
Your heart captured mine
And the universe spoke
Together you shine

You told me your name
Before I arrived
As if knowing the plan
Would make me come alive

You did heal my heart
And I healed yours
And from that moment
Came more open doors

So here is to more
Adventures and love
More cuddles and hugs
Just a dog and her Dove

Maiden & the Knight

Essence of Love

Billowy clouds
Waves on the shore
Touching a rainbow
Remembering life from before

Glancing within
Glancing without
Honoring the soul
What the path is about

Essence of Love
All around and within
Like cotton candy
Enjoying the whim

Love feeds the soul
Expands like the tides
It ebbs and flows
And once found never hides

That grain of sand
On the glistening beach
Blends in with the rest
Pure union it seeks

The union is bliss
The pure essence of love
The soul finds its answers
Preset from above

Oh yes it is there
The answer thus found
I cry out in Joy
Essence of love abounds

Encounters

Not known at the time
How long it would be
That our paths would stay crossed
And what was needed to be
Some encounters can last
A lifetime you see
And some are quite short
When it's time to leave
Once the lesson is learned
Of the business at hand
We take that gift with us
And on both feet we land
We take the next step
And we're never the same
As we all once were
Before those encounters came
Each one is unique
Many awesome gifts
Makes the spirit soar
And helps the soul uplift
At times it is sad
When encounters depart
But souls were connected
Thereby touching the heart

Exquisite

One touch of your hand
Brings such a glow
Touches deeply my heart
Straight into my soul

How blessed am I
To be gifted such love
I hear them say ah!
And watch them smile from above

Like billowy clouds
And waves rippling to shore
We've done this forever
So many times before

The tears flow so free
The dance vivid and wild
Like blowing bubbles
As if like a child

You move into me
I move into you
The union is bliss
And the love so true

The comfort you bring
Like a fire when cold
The heat brings the warmth
What a caress to behold!

You are right here
By my side
You know all of me
There's nothing to hide

I'm there with you
Returning the fire
Each time we meet
We soar higher and higher

Up into the rainbow
We dance tenderly
Embracing our souls
Then we sit and just be

There are no words
To describe such a feeling
But a knowing within
Sends the heart reeling

Perhaps such a word
Could try and come close
That word is exquisite
Embraced by a rose

Feel me today
I'm right there with you
And know what I'm feeling
Is pure love so true

Send me a smile
And a hug in reply
Let's join our wings
Today we shall fly

Tin Man

Alone in the forest
Rusted and stiff from rain
Awaiting true love
To open your heart once again

You say when they made you
They forgot the heart
But it's always been there
And never apart

I bring forth the oil
Cleaning away all the rust
My love rings so true
Of that you can trust

No need to find Oz
Searching all from without
It's right there within you
Of that please don't doubt

Although dormant from rain
Once was so very alive
Reawakens in glory
And continues to thrive

Trust that it's there
For all Eternity
Let the cleansing oil
Once again set it free

Share with me now
The yellow brick road
We shall walk it together
And lessen the load

Not to seek the wizard
For the answer is within
But to find the rainbow
And to live once again

It shines above Oz
The emerald sea
Forever to guide us
And allow us to see

That returning home
Along this path
Is inside the heart
Truly a rainbow bath

The castle of Oz
Grows deep within
Emerald and golden
And I allow you in

The Touch

Like a gentle breeze
It caresses my face
Waves wash over me
And I'm at a new place

Whispers of love
Dancing around me with glee
And sparkles of light
All around me I see

It quickens my heart
And embraces with wings
I'm bathed in the warmth
And the soul truly sings

Transcending all time
It is not of this place
But of the stars
Taking away all heartache

The dance of the touch
Is celestial bliss
Joining with moonbeams
And a rainbow's kiss

Sparkle

Sparkle of your eyes

Sunshine in your smile

Do I dare reach out

and hold you for awhile

We met one day

Not too long ago

I knew it was fate

Your smile told me so

You reached with your hand

And touched my heart

That one loving caress

Said, we've never been apart

Sparkle of your eyes

Sunshine in your smile

Do I dare reach out

And hold you for awhile

We've met before

Somewhere in time

I know this is true

From the light that shines

The sparkle is there

And will always stay

Bringing whispers of love

And smiles each day

Sparkle of your eyes

Sunshine in your smile

Do I dare reach out

And hold you for awhile

Moonlight Dance

Sparkles of love
Fill the air
It comes so sudden
Just out of nowhere

The dance begins
From deep within
Two hearts are joined
Floating on a whim

Fireflies join
Butterflies too
Then rainbows appear
With awesome hues

Dancing on air
Soul to soul
Holding close
Basking in the glow

Not of this earth
But spiritual love
Two hearts join as one
Increasing love from above

This joining in spirit
Brings Memories clear
Through sands of time
Erasing all fear

The dance is bliss
Stirring the heart
Explodes in passion
Waves of ecstasy start

Ripples cascade
Flowing and free
Reaching other souls
Throughout eternity

This dance of Love
In the moonlight glow
Brings forth changes
Connecting all souls

Oh yes it is bliss
And part of the plan
This dance of Love
Thru eternity spans

Come dance with me now
Our hearts shall soar
Feeling sparkles of fire
Bringing ripples galore

Sending them out
For all to feel
And so at your heart
I lovingly kneel

Song of Love

The cooing dove

Sits in my tree

Is joined by sparrow

Such a melody

I awaken each day

Hearing their song

They sing of love

And I know I belong

What others may miss

I seek and find

The song it does touch

This heart of mine

The soul cries its tears

Of joy and glee

And with this song

My soul stays free

To seek and grow

And send forth love

Remaining aware

Of the connection above

It grows as a flower

It flows like the stream

It sparkles of light

Dancing on sunbeams

This song I shall carry

Spread forth to all souls

Thanking God for the gifts

And I bask in the glow

The Flame

The flame, the fire
Brings eternal desire
Soul joins to soul
Casting a rainbow glow

Feel it within
Brings heat to the skin
Feel it without
Sends forth a shout

Pure joy is the song
Oh yes we belong
Eternal connection
A candy confection

Sweetness of Love
Takes flight above
Past stars at night
Shining so bright

Reaching the rainbow
Such colors, such glow
Dancing moonbeams
Opens heaven it seems

Sending golden sunshine
And sparks so divine
Flame burns so deep
Eternal love to keep

Joining as one
Melting into the sun
Song of love
Sent forth from above

Breath of Passion

Icy hot
Filling the lungs
Reaching the soul
Never to stop

Floating in love
Fueling the flame
Explodes in the sky
Fire shoots from above

Heat it does bring
In waves it comes
Steam rising to top
Making the soul sing

Orange in hues
Outlined in purple
Waterfalls of pink
Clouds of bright blues

Song of bliss
As the siren sings
It's all about love
Sealed with a kiss

Hands of love
Touching my waist
Holding so tight
I feel the hug

The passion, the heat,
Is a song of love
Like cotton candy
It tastes so sweet

The Maiden and the Knight

She sat high in her prison tower pondering the situation, surrounded by the harsh walls of her reality. Would she stay forever imprisoned, or would she be relieved of her burden? The hawk has circled for two days now, bringing her the message that yes indeed, her knight in shining armor would arrive soon to rescue her.

On the third day, to her excitement, she heard the pounding of a horse's hooves and knew her mate had come to save her. She glanced outside her window perched ever so high and was quite stunned at what she was witnessing. Yes, it was a knight, but the armor was not at all shining and in fact showed signs of rust. How could this be?

She closed her eyes and reached out with her heart and soul to discover that this was indeed her knight in shining armor. She called out to him, "You are not quite the shining knight I saw in my vision so I shall nickname you Tin Man, for you are in need of an oil can. Now if you would be so kind as to come up here and rescue your fair maiden whereby we may ride off into the sunset and live happily ever after."

He was indeed so very handsome she thought, rust and all and as he grinned up at her, his light shown for what seemed miles around him. Her heart began to pick up speed and the heat increased. To her shock and amazement his words cut deep into her heart and soul, shattering her every being. "I would indeed so love to climb up there and rescue you my dear sweet beloved but alas, I cannot."

What? What was this? The maiden yelled out, "Explain yourself."

"My dear sweet beloved, I am instructed not to rescue you although it tears my heart and soul apart. It is your quest to break free from your own imprisonment. You must rescue yourself and set your soul free."

This was not at all the fairy tale told to her for years as a young woman growing up. She was baffled at this. The next thing she knew her Knight said, "I now must take my leave of you my dear beloved for I have my own journey to attend to and perhaps we shall meet up again one day."

What the hell was this? She had sat there waiting and praying for her knight to come and rescue her and now her dream had vanished. She would stay imprisoned and forever die of loneliness she thought. He blew her a kiss, grinning ever so wickedly, and at that point she wished she had something to throw at him! The gall! How dare he ride off and leave her this way, with nothing left to hope for. She felt so abandoned, so very alone. She heard him singing ever so gallantly as he strode off with his horse. Although infuriated with him, she had to admit his voice was so melodious, so sweet, and so sensual it stayed with her soothing her very soul.

She allowed herself the anger, the rage, the frustration of her sense of abandonment. In the midst of the anger, came an awakening. The awakening was of the magnitude of a huge rainbow which burst through after a harsh storm, shedding joy and light and vivid colors across the sky!

I will do this; I will show him and the world that I can indeed free myself from these walls. She called upon the inner strength she never knew was inside her. Her thoughts became a frenzied plan of accomplishment. She went into a very deep meditation in which to find the answer and the way out of her dilemma. The realization came suddenly, as fast as a shooting star across the night. She knew then that she could do something which had always been available to her but remained hidden until her soul was ready. The excitement was beyond describing, the rush of pure joy cascading through every pore of her being.

She prepared herself mentally, spiritually, and emotionally. This took some time although she knew the outcome would be positive and her patience was needed.

When she was ready, she stood at the window of the tower, the ground loomed ever so menacingly yet she was no longer afraid. She closed her eyes, breathing in the dawn of the new day within her lungs, spread her wings, and flew. The flight was effortless, filled with such sheer ecstasy, feeling the wind in her face, as if merging with it. The sky began to fill with the most iridescent rainbow she had ever seen, along with birds soaring, and the melodious sound of angels' voices singing.

The landing was smooth and touching down she felt light as a feather. She looked up to where she had once been imprisoned, the tall tower, the walls of concrete, the fortress of pain. At that moment the walls of the tower crumbled, crushing down all around and turned into a garden of roses and baby's breath. She knew she had conquered something that took much courage and faith and patience. Her soul sang with the knowledge that she rescued herself; a knowing that no one else could have done so but her. It was her choice and her path to do alone. She danced along her path, moving forward and wondering what new journey would now await her. She sang a song of freedom and love and joy. The birds joined in along with the animals of the woods.

Sometime later she looked up ahead on her path and strained her eyes to see what it could be. As she got closer, she saw him. Oh my God! How can this be? But it was true; there he was sitting on a large rock and singing yet another melodious, sensual tune. Her Knight! But what is this? No longer was he rusty and needing oiled. His armor was shining, polished and glistened in the sun. What had happened to him?

When he saw her approach, his smile had a knowing look. Their eyes connected and somehow she knew the answer. "My beloved," he said. "I wanted to rescue you, this you must know but I knew I could not do so. You had to do your own work and release yourself from your prison. I in turn had my own work and journey to do while you had yours. I have been waiting for you. I knew you would persevere and break down the walls of that fortress and come to me."

She then understood that his new shining armor came as a result of his hard work, conquering his own burden and one he had to do alone, just as she had to do hers alone. He came to her then, embraced her, gently kissed the palms of her hands, and said "You are a song of love."

Once again reunited, the Maiden and her Knight knew that no matter what came they could conquer all. Their separate journeys had proved this. Together they would stay for all eternity, loving, sharing, enduring, and co-creating together. He helped her to mount onto the horse, getting on behind her, arms around her waist, holding her strongly. She was comforted in his embrace, knowing no harm could now ever befall her. They rode off into the sunset and lived happily ever after.

Bring Me a Flower

A single rose
Touches the lips
Scented with love
Moonlight eclipse

Caresses the heart
Stirs the soul
Just one brings
A radiant glow

No need for more
One brings a smile
Of eternal love
And I drift for awhile

Silky and soft
Across my face
Brightens the eyes
Fills me with grace

Tears of Joy
Surround me in love
With a tender kiss
And a rainbow hug

In Spirit

Across the distance

Seems so far away

And I sit and wonder

Where you are today

To hear your words

I long for so dear

Perhaps one day

It will all become clear

Although there are miles

Keeping us apart

I still feel the hugs

And the love in your heart

Though trusting the plan

Seems so hard at times

I then get a rainbow

And with it sunshine

Hawk still comes to me

Each day in the sky

To remind me of love

And I breathe with a sigh

The signs are all there

They won't let me forget

That the bond will not sever

Since the day we first met

I reach out in love

And send you a smile

And sit in the quiet

To hold you awhile

Flamenco Fire

Colors burst forth
Explodes out from the heart
cascading into brilliant hues
sending ripples to the soul
of wonder and chills
makes the feet want to dance
and the voice to sing

Your love of life
shows thru the words

Your caring heart
for the wee small ones
shows as the brilliant rainbow
cascading down on their souls

Fiery red glows as the flame
a flame of pure love
for the song, the music, for life
and for the children

Your blessings abound
It shows in your music
It shows in your soul

Flight of the Goddess

She stands at the edge
Pondering her life
Her heart calls her to act
Yet her mind stands in fear
Take the leap she hears
Your wings will carry you
Yet her feet remain still
Not moving, frozen, anchored
Yet she knows on the horizon
Something awaits her

And it's magnificent, this she knows
Do it my sweet, take the leap
The whispers continue
Now is the time
She sees the light, it's so bright
Slowly her feet move
Her passion explodes
She spreads her wings
And soars to her destiny

Goddess on Fire

She is a Goddess of fire and passion
The embers glow just beneath the surface
Lying in wait; a volcano preparing to erupt
Building over time, unable to stop the
explosion
For she must release her passion, her fire
within
She waits for the time, for the "one"
She is not to erupt before then
She must lie in wait, preparing as in birth
Simmering as a broth brews
Slowly as if making a stew
A stew of love, passion, fire and heat

Her petals await the time to bloom
Her fragrance to permeate the earth
Cascading in her own perfume
The scent intoxicating and on fire
The burning passion of heat
The burning passion of love
The burning passion of desire

She waits, not to be devoured
But to be savored, loved and adored
Her temple is sacred

Her love is pure
Her heart is a flower
Opened and ready
Her scent is of the ocean
Her love is as the rainbow
Her passion is as the stars
Bursting forth in the sky
Her desire is as the moon
Ebbing and flowing with the tide
Her heart is as the sun
Shooting forth heat and light

She waits, this Goddess
Preparing to burst forth from her temple
When her beloved calls
And their union becomes one
One with the cosmos
One with each other
Sending ripples in the afterglow

Adventures

If you want my heart, softly whisper in my
ear

But if you want to join my soul, take me on
an adventure

Not just any adventure, one that feeds the
wildness within me

Taking risks as we go, laughing at the
craziness of it all

Let's feel the wind, ride the wild highways
of life

And feel the passion within each of our
spirits

Passion, ah, yes, that is what drives me in
life

Show me the passion that drives you wild

And I will show you the passion that drives
me wild

*Catching the sunset over the canyon, or a
beach*

Admiring the beauty of a sunrise each day

*That ignites the fire within, bursting forth
in flames*

Yes, you can still whisper softly in my ear

*But do it with   passion so that my ears
feel and taste it*

*I will then share not only my heart, but my
soul*

*I will send you ripples of smiles and
laughter*

I will dance with wild abandon

And we will live and love in the moment

For now is all we have

Let's do this

Travels of Otter Woman

Spirit Helpers

One day there appeared
In front of my face
One large dragonfly
Buzzing as if in a race
I show you illusions
And remind you to see
To look past the façade
Not door one, two, but door three

The next day came spider
Weaving her web
I remind you to create
Even when life seems to ebb
Expand your horizon
And make it grow
Weave it so strong
And thus it will glow

And then deer arrived
Just at the right time
Saying be gentle with you
As your light always shines
Don't be so hard
To critique those flaws
They help you to grow

And learn Universal Law

And when wolf arrived
So ready to teach
I opened my eyes
Such truth did I seek
He knew I was ready
To learn a new phase
To take the next step
Moving me forward a ways

And then time to rest
When otter appeared
He taught me to play
And with applause he cheered
We danced and we sang
And giggled with glee
And so otter taught me
How to become carefree

I wonder which one
Will come to me now
I keep my eyes open
And always allow
They each make me ponder
Each step of the way
On this path called life
What more can I say

I bid them to come
Teach me something new
This I will then share
As we are all meant to do

Earth Dance

Dancing free
Hands held high
Embracing spirit
Touching the sky

Caressing the Earth
With thanks and Love
Joining in circle
With Creator above

My Spirit rejoicing
To help Mother Earth
For she has done wonders
In giving birth

She sends us beauty
Each day to see
A river to soothe us
To sit and just be

She gives her love
With a simple blink
It does cause me to wonder
To stop, sit and think

Do we love in return?
Show her respect?
Without healing and love
What can we expect?

Let's give back to her
What she gives to us all
When she cries out her tears
Let's heed the call

It's time to unite
Help heal Mother Earth
And by doing this
Can cause a rebirth

Of love, of life
Of healing and caring
By joining in love
All hearts will be sharing

Let's join as One
And set our intent
To help Our Mother
Who from Heaven was sent

Give back to her
The love she gives
In showing respect
Her heart will forgive

Forbidden Love

In the darkness of the night,
underneath a moon shining its glow
near the tree blooming so full,
the river flowing by in quiet harmony,
the lovers embrace.
This man holding so passionately,
this woman responding in ecstasy.

There is fear.
How many nights has this fear come?
With each secret embrace and kiss
comes the fear of being seen.

The lovers eternally bound in soul,
yet not to be in this lifetime.
How many lifetimes has their love been
forbidden?

Her long cape blows in the wind.
His embrace holds her steady and calm.
His kiss ignites the fire as a flame lights the
coals.
The coals burn steady, never fading away,
but lingering with the heat,
Steady, hot and explosive.

Waiting for the time when there is no need
to hide, to openly express their desires,
their joined heat.

The times are few and they must take
when they can, loving each other from afar
when in the presence of others.
The yearning so strong, the tears flow.
Tears overflowing like a dam bursting,
unable to be stopped or tamed.

She bids her love yet another farewell
until the next clandestine meeting.
He embraces her yet again, declaring his
love, a last passionate kiss between lovers.

She moves back along the river, through
the trees,
ever so quiet so as not to disturb the world.

She retreats to her sitting area,
allowing only quiet tears to flow,
still feeling his kiss and his strong embrace.

The Travels of Otter Woman

She sat by the river taking her mid-morning rest. She had been walking so very far and had farther yet to go this day. What a lovely place to sit and be still she thought. Vivid colors all around her, the emerald green of the grassy meadow, the rich browns, yellows, and purples of the trees showing fall had arrived, and across the river, a cascading water fall amidst flowers of red, blue, and peach. The air was crisp and alive. A butterfly lazily drifted by, huge and beckoning. Her otter friends soon appeared, just as she knew they would. This time it was a couple, playful and happy, carefree and simple, a reminder to stop a while and play, enjoying the earth.

Winter will arrive soon and she must prepare, but for now, this day, she sits among the beauty of Mother Earth, resting within her breast, breathing in life. Her meditative thoughts drift back, back to younger days. She was destined at birth to become a healer. Her teacher and mentor arrived at the appointed time while she was in her maidenhood years; teaching her all he knew. There was much to learn, the gathering of the right herbs, how and when to use them, and her studies of all healing modalities. Her inner work to prepare as healer was strict and required much discipline. He was a Master, one she aspired to become one day.

It was he who told her, "You are called to be a Healer. There is much expected of you and the heart, mind, and body must be purified and remain so. The love must come from deep within the heart. You will journey to many lands as guided. Your life as healer will at times be a lonely one, for you travel solo, and this is necessary. Do not get too attached to anyone or any place. Self-sacrifice and discipline are needed as healer. Your purpose is to help others."

A loud splash brought her back to the present. The otter friends gleefully teased each other, playing as if children having a new toy for the first time. She was glad to see them this day. The otters reminded her to take time for her play and to enjoy all the beauty around her. The otters came closer, peering with cheerful eyes. Kindred souls she and they were. Her teacher named her Otter woman because although she was a serious student and desired to learn all she could as healer, she also enjoyed playing near the water in her spare time, when not in her studies with the Master. Her teacher observed the otters coming to visit her each time she entered the pool of water for bathing or just simply to swim.

Her birth name given was White Dove and indeed that was her spirit. She relished her given name as well as the Otter woman her teacher chose as her healer name. Her doves fly above her, her otters swim next to her.

Her latest destination came to her in a dream. Her healing was needed she was told, and she was shown the village. Her steps as always were guided by Spirit. She knew that her arrival time would be synchronistic, in tune. The load she carried was always one of lightness, gathering herbs as she went. Her medicine pouch she always carried. She was of no particular tribe except what she called the "rainbow tribe." This tribe has many cultures, peoples, and races. All are dedicated to healing and helping others, including Mother Earth. As she recalls this, her eyes are drawn to the sky. She smiled with warmth and love as she saw the signs appear: the vibrant wondrous double rainbow with the two hawks soaring among it.

She is then overcome with a love so deep, a heat so passionate, her soul burns with fire! This sign is her reminder that she was deeply, deeply, loved and protected and thought of. There is a merging of energies, her thoughts reach out, reach out to him, the one who holds her heart, soul and eternal love. He is her twin flame, her other essence, who shares her soul, as he has for all eternity. This bond will never be broken.

His name is Hawk and his spirit soars in the hawks just as hers soars in the white doves. Their shared love of rainbows began at the beginning of time, when they were created. The hawk and the dove soar together among twin rainbows. His journey takes him elsewhere, to other lands and peoples. He too is healer and must follow his calling as does she. Their souls are joined as a melting flame. They are as one. Though miles apart in distance, he is yet near and she feels him always. He sends his love, his protection, his heat. And oh what heat! She feels the arms around her and the gentle caresses. It is a hard journey to be so separated in the physical with her Beloved, but their lives are destined so. Their face-to-face visits are always short and sweet and far between, but they make the most of them.

She realizes it is best not to dwell on that at the moment. Sometimes the pain is too deep. She smiles then as she bids the otters farewell. Her break and rest is now over and it is time to go forward on her path so as to be at the village at precisely the appointed time. This journey would only take three days, shorter than most.

Leaving behind the playful otters, she looks up ahead. The beauty of Mother Earth continues to astound her. The faraway mountains, the hues, the shimmers, the sky so very blue, crystal clear, touches her soul. The rainbow remains in the sky, along with the hawks. The smile remains not only on her lips, but in her heart; her beloved hugging her from a distance. She proceeds on her journey. Just as planned, she reaches the edge of the village on the evening of the third day. As usual, she announces her arrival by sounding her drum. She always carries this with her as part of her entourage. The resounding drumbeat back confirms they are awaiting her and the greeting is a welcome feeling. Her feet were getting weary and she longed to sit awhile and rest the soul, and longed for a bath. The smoke from the village smells of cooking and the laughter of children playing brought warmth to her heart and a smile to her soul.

She was greeted by the Elders. Her arrival had been given in a vision to the Chief Elder. Many prayers had been given to Great Spirit asking for healing of the small boy who had become ill of unknown origin. The village was vibrant and alive with energy. She was already tuning in, sensing the emotional state of the village. All had concerns for this child, this member of their community. However, she could also sense their faith and trust in Great Spirit. This was the vibrant energy she felt.

The village greeted her with hope and strength. Time was of the essence and she took only a short time in which to rest, refresh and to prepare herself. She did this by entering the sweat lodge and praying to

Creator. This was to purify her as well as connect with Spirit.

When she was ready, she gathered with the elders, family, and the young boy whose name was Walks with Deer. She was informed that he was a very gentle being, who could call the deer and they would come to him. His gentle nature was felt by all in the village and his love spread to each and every member there. Never was there an angry word spoken from his lips. Many of the village looked to him as a role model for their own behavior, even though he was but a small child. They felt Creator had big plans for this little one, if only he would survive this illness.

All preparations were complete. After the purifying, cleansing, smudging and prayers, she proceeded on. The boy's fever was quite high and his bed was soaked from the sweating. She gently placed her hands over the boy, calling upon Great Spirit and the Universal Healing Energy. All true healers know that they are strictly the open channel, the vessel for which the healing flows through. The healing comes from Spirit always. She was intensely focused and opened herself to allow this healing to flow through. There was no need to rush, it was all in Divine Timing, and the healing would flow as long as needed and would flow to where it was needed. She sensed it was not a life threatening illness, and saw the infection flow throughout his body.

She closed her eyes, placing her hands where guided and set her intent for the healing. Her body became a hot furnace, her hands beet red as the energy began to flow. Eventually the boy's breathing became calmer; his body began to loosen from the tension and became somewhat cooler to the touch. Time seemed to go on forever, although in reality it was but a short time. When Spirit guided her to do so, she slowly began to refocus, and step back from the flowing of the energy. She knew the healing had done what was needed and the young boy would recover. She prayed to Great Spirit and gave thanks for the honor of being given this gift of healer. She sat quietly for a while and remained connected with the boy. It is always amazing that although healing is being sent forth to the one needing it, the healer gets it in return and she felt renewed, refreshed and an energy burst through her every being. She was not tired or drained, but alive with vibrant joy!

She informed the family that he would slowly recover and that his fever would break soon. The relief on the faces of his mother and father, along with gratitude, made her heart soar with Love. This is her purpose, her passion, her true calling. Each and every time she was called to do healing, it always brought her pure joy. It was her yearning, her heart's desire to help others on their path. It made her humble; as it did each and every time she was asked to do healing work.

Since she always fasted before healing work, she was now famished and ready to eat. The village had made quite a feast in honor of her coming and the food was plenty. The songs sung as well as the dancing were full of joy and happiness. When notified that the young boy's fever had indeed broken, the ceremony jubilantly increased and she sat in awe as she always does after a healing. Her favorite dance was performed. The small children always made her smile, especially when they danced the eagle dance, wearing their wardrobe of brilliant eagle feathers, colored head dresses and used their rattles.

It was a dance done with reverence and the colors displayed from the children splashed across the sky like a myriad of rainbows. The entire circle was alive and vibrant with fiery energy, and the drummers all came alive and their music was vibrating like thunder crashing across the sky. She smiled so widely and in prayer opened her arms to the heavens and gave thanks yet again. She joined in with her own drum and felt the heartbeat of Mother Earth. The village was a very kind and loving people. She was well taken care of and overwhelmed with the sheer joy and appreciation shown.

She had been given a lovely area in which to sleep and rest up for her return trip home. The next morning she greeted the four directions at sunrise. The brilliant red orange glow of the rising sun always made her soul soar. She was informed the young boy Walks with Deer was sitting up and taking liquids. She went to greet him and his light shown so bright and his heart was full of love and joy.

She saw his future and he was destined to also be a healer. A healer recognizes another kindred healer. Their eyes connected and no words were spoken but each knew one another and the purpose they shared on this earthly walk. She knew his teacher would come at the appointed time to help him with his walk, just as hers had come. She stayed two days and then it was time to embark on her return journey. The village gave her bundles of wrapped food and drink to take with her. As healer she does not ask for any payment. However, the parents wished to gift a very beautiful necklace of turquoise and fine pearls. This she would accept and it was placed around her neck. It felt most warm near her heart and she was honored with such a gift.

She bid them all farewell promising to return another time. She knew she would encounter this young boy again and she looked forward to doing so. The sun was high into the sky when she started her return journey.

Walking along her heart skipped a beat as she knew she would soon see her beloved for a few uninterrupted days of alone time. She felt him draw her near and wrap his wings around her in comfort, and felt his love deep within her heart. She looked to the sky to see her hawk soaring into the rainbow, calling out to his beloved, "Come to me."

She quickened her steps and headed up the path, singing a song of love and joy, knowing her beloved awaited her.

Meadow Reunion

Among the meadow of golden hues

A myriad of wings, all color in flight

Exploding into a billion light specks

At once the field blooms into a milky way

Rainbow showers across the sky

Cascading down to become butterflies

Dancing on air, surrounding the maiden

She opens her arms to encompass it all

Warmth spreading through her soul

Shooting sparks of ember glow

The meadow becomes one with her

A blanket of warmth soothing the heart

Merging together brings purple hues

Like lavender fields spreading out for miles

The purple then joined by buttercups

Milky yellow and soft to the touch

She closes her eyes, reaching out to him

They merge once again like a sparrow on wind

His spirit arrives to join with hers

Together they soar to their place in the clouds

Only for them, a place of pure love

Two beloveds embrace, reunion such bliss

Written on the song of eternal love

The union is one, the passion explodes

Sending a golden flame to Heaven and Earth

Remembering You

Kisses that linger
unfolding as the searing heat,
melting the river, flowing, cascading,
embraced in the afterglow of pure light,
golden sunshine engulfing you, warming
me.
Together forever, eternally, this we knew,
would always know we are one . . .

Yet to go our separate ways thru each
lifetime, having a sense of each other, the
longing, the heartache.
Yet knowing, knowing, you are out there,
and I am here.
The reminders remain, always there to
weave the tapestry
of remembrance, of eternal bonds of love,
flames of fire,
the heat, the intense sensations warming
and engulfing the soul.
Yes, it is you, deep, deep within and inside
of me, forever merged,
forever joined . . . .

Family

The Family Nobody Wanted

Eric got to school, along with his two little sisters who were a grade and two grades behind him. At 11-years old he felt much older than his young age, having had to watch out for his sisters for a few years now. After his dad lost his job and his mom had gotten sick, they eventually were forced to live in and out of shelters. It was certainly better than the old station wagon they lived out of for six months. His dad George finally got a job but his mom with her health, although better, couldn't seem to find work. So many people; so many judgments.

His mom had AIDs from a blood transfusion she had after giving birth to the youngest child. Through no fault of her own she was treated like a leper. In fact it was as if they were the family nobody wanted. At least the stigma of AIDs didn't carry over into the school arena, but most knew that the children were homeless and the relentless teasing from a couple of the bullies made it at times a tough situation. Thank God the AIDs was not a part of the bullying, it would have made things more unbearable to attend school.

The teachers were kind though, and so were the principal and the school counselor. Eric had high hopes of wanting to become a doctor after he witnessed what his mother had gone through. He shared this dream with the school counselor and his teacher who were both very encouraging to him. In fact they gave him extra assignments so that his education could give him more of a boost and get him prepared. He studied hard and mainly kept to himself. He wanted to be around his mom and help her out the best he could while his dad worked.

He was a loner and didn't make friends easily. He kept his nose to the grindstone and during recess read his books while he kept his eyes on his sisters playing across the playground. At least they didn't feel the pressure of the world and the homelessness as much as he did. They seemed happy and content.

One day Eric met a new resident at the shelter. He was an older man who appeared to be well kept and clean. He seemed out of place at the shelter, yet there he was. He was a very friendly man who seemed genuinely interested in all the families there and their stories. Eric sat off in the corner of their small section watching the man with a keen interest in what he was saying. Several times the man looked in his direction and Eric quickly averted his eyes. The man eventually ended up near Eric and his family and asked to sit down and enjoy the dinner meal with them. His dad and mom were gracious and said yes.

Eric began to really like this mysterious fellow who wanted to know all about everyone else without sharing who he was. He asked Eric what he wanted to be when he grew up to which Eric replied, "A doctor." This brought a huge grin from the older gentlemen who seemed to have a twinkle in his eye at Eric's response. As the parents shared the story of their plight, the older man, who we later found out was named Greg, was deeply disturbed by how the family had been treated during this period of time and had a genuine caring.

Over the next week or so, Eric began to look forward to seeing Greg as they would sit down and have discussions about life and what Eric truly had a passion for. In fact the whole shelter enjoyed Greg and always wanted him to sit at their area of the table for dinner, but for some reason he always chose Eric's family.

After a month had passed, one day Greg did not arrive to the shelter and everyone, Including Eric truly missed seeing him. One day turned into a week and everyone became sad and wondered if Greg was alright. On the 8th day during dinner time, a commotion was going on outside the shelter with loud noises. Everyone got up and began to look through the windows. They saw one of the biggest limousines they had ever seen! In fact there were motorcycle cops in front and in back of it. That must have been the noise.

All of a sudden the door to the limo opened and out walked a regal looking gentleman in a fancy suit, carrying a briefcase, and escorted by an entourage. On close inspection they realized it was Greg! As Greg entered the shelter, everyone was so stunned, they couldn't speak a word. He walked to the front of the shelter where announcements were given and took the Mic. He began to share his "real" story of how he was homeless as a youngster, and went on to become the business man he was today. He had vowed to give back to those whom he felt a strong connection; the homeless. He made a huge donation to the shelter but that wasn't the biggest surprise. He turned to Eric's family, asking them to come forward. Greg stated how impressed he was with all of them and how they stuck together and took care of each other. Not only did he give Eric's mom a job at his company, he also set up a trust for when Eric and his sisters were ready for college. The trust would pay their tuition.

Then the BIG surprise! Greg had a home all ready for the family to move into immediately. Eric's mom cried, his dad was humbled, and Eric sat quiet , thinking to himself, *When I become an adult, that's exactly what I am going to do; just what this Greg did*. He would pay it forward and help the homeless.

That's exactly what Eric did when he became a doctor years later. He helped and cared for the sick in the homeless shelters.

Reclaiming the Milky Way

Was a long time ago
I sat as a child
Peered up into the night
And at once felt so wild
I wanted to be
In the midst of it all
It meant freedom to me
Like heeding the call
It sprang forth so vast
Across miles to be seen
It called out my name
Such light did it gleam
It sparkled like glitter
Shimmering bright in the sky
Thereby lighting the dark
And it made my soul cry
The tears were of joy
Of love and of bliss
Reminding me of home
Which was so very missed

Yet still I felt cradled

And loved, yes indeed
Each night it was there
Each night I felt free
And then thru the years
It became harder to see
As if darkness took over
And I felt much less free
The Earth had so changed
Did that cause it to flee?
And even less stars
In the sky did I see
I call you back
And ask with a plea
Please return to the sky
Once again, set me free
So I close my eyes
Once again I'm a child
Reclaiming that feeling
And am cradled awhile
The image is there
Etched in my memory
And by closing my eyes
Allows me to see
The shimmer, the light
Such a vast galaxy
And within it the love
Ah, once again . . . ecstasy

David and Beth

He struggles to walk
Takes one step at a time
It's hard to talk
But his words always shine

She sits in a wheelchair
Confined there since birth
But each day she's happy
To be here on Earth

They gaze at each other
Their love so pure
They are devoted
Of this I'm quite sure

Although Life gives them this
They return love tenfold
To watch them together
What a site to behold

Although her limbs
She's unable to use
The artwork she creates
Ah, the magic, the hues

Their gifts bring a smile
They both feel so blessed
Although each day of their lives
Is always a test

No matter what comes
Each day they do smile
And I always get healing
Sitting with them awhile

I count my blessings
For having met these two
They show me true love
And how each day I can choose

To start with a smile
Or send out a frown
To send forth love to all
Or to choose to be down

And so by their love
A reminder to me
I choose the smile
And set my heart free

Legs of Steel

Legs of Steel

Life always amazes me and each day I look for magic. Sometimes it comes easily, sometimes the magic brings with it painful memories, but it is magic nonetheless.

I felt the need to begin to clean out old boxes in my closet and came upon some poems I had no idea I had even written. I am unsure of the date for the one I share today. Along with the poem I found some old pictures of me; the ones I used to hide from people so they couldn't comment on how sad it must have been to be crippled as a child. I didn't need that painful reminder, the memories of being teased and taunted, ridiculed and made fun of.

For a brief moment those painful memories returned and then I chose to replace them with this phrase, "Aw, but you got strength from it also." With my braces I learned to walk without crutches. They were put away and I refused to use them. I held my own in dealing with those who were mean to me. I learned it from my Mama, I saw her lash out at those who made fun of her precious lil' child (thank you Mama!). That's what moms do.

It was only a year or so of having to wear them but I was unable to put my legs together the entire time. I tell ya that is not an easy thing for a child to deal with, let alone a Mother who was also pregnant and having to help care for me. But she did it from Love and I felt it.

I added a title as when I saw the pics again, the words Legs of Steel came. I share it with you, unedited. Somehow by sharing this, I get even more healing and release from old painful memories. My brother and grandmother are with me in the pic. The second pic is of me and some of my siblings.

I once knew a girl so full of life
And then by chance it was filled with strife
Her once active legs were divided by steel
This is not what you'd call a happy ordeal
Her mother so lovely, her family so dear
Couldn't help to shed her many tears
She was known as a freak, not like others
at all
And because of her shame couldn't walk
very tall
Then after what seemed an eternity
She shed her steel and was finally free
Her family so happy, this girl full of gleam
Began to run and to laugh and to scream
At the joy of her freedom from this bar of
steel
Her life had been freed from this sordid
ordeal
Her life was then changed from sad to
gleeful
She no longer shied away from other
people
Though now she is grown and her legs are
well healed
Shell never forget that sordid ordeal
This girl I once knew is now happy and free
And I ought to know

FOR THAT GIRL IS ME!

And Now I Can Dance

You stood in my way
And I wanted to dance
To move like the wind
To take that big chance

I listened to you
Accepting your words
Thereby stopping the movement
To dance? How absurd!

But deep down inside
I knew this untrue
Why did I listen?
Making me so down and blue

What is it I love
Most of all?
To move with the dance
Even if I fall

Your words are untrue
And I reclaim the chance
I bless and release you
And now I can dance

I Want You

I want you to live your life
I want you take full flight
I want you to spread your Wings
I want you to always sing
I want you to find your gift
I want you to no longer drift
I want you to find your passion
Whatever it takes, whatever fashion
I want you to search inside
I want you to no longer hide
I want you to know you are loved
I want you to feel when hugged
I want you to know it is okay
To sometimes fall on a given day
I want you to get back up
I want you to refill the cup
I want you to see what I see
I want you to be all you can be
I want you to always love You
Just like God and I now do
I want you to find inner peace
The pain within to be released
I want you to reach out to me
Hand in hand, feeling so free

Hello God

Hello God, it's me, remember?
I know it's been awhile
I want to ask a favor
See Mommy and daddy
Are very sick
It is those pills I think
Maybe that place they are at now
Will help them to get well
It wasn't really them that hurt me
It was the pills
I know deep down they love me
Don't they?
I am asking you to help them
To get well
And to love me again

I am cared for here
I am loved here and fed
But they are not my parents
I get hugs and kisses
And we play games
But I cry at night
For it is not my home
I wonder if they cry at night

For me
Like I do for them
They do love me don't they?

I know you do very much
I can always count on you
But I want my mommy and daddy
To come and get me
And take me home
And be a family

My bruises are healing
And my black eye too
I forgive them,
I always do
No matter what
I love them
Don't they see that?

Will you please tell them that?
And help them get well
So I can go home
And be loved?

Thank you God!

A lonely child who seeks love

Listening to the
Inner Voice

Listening to the Inner Voice

In the very beginning of my work with hospice patients, I encountered a retired vet who had been struggling with his illness. I got him to open up about his flying days in the military and we began to have a unique connection. I called him Yogi Bear and he called me Boo Boo. After a short time his condition worsened and I was informed he was taken to one of the units.

Later that evening I had gone to see another patient at a different unit. I had worked later into the evening and as I was heading home, I felt a strong pull to visit my retired vet. I realized I was going to be going right by the unit where he was staying. I struggled with this as I didn't wish to intrude on any family time. However, the pull was so strong I made a decision to stop in.

Upon entering the room, I was greeted by his daughter who I had spoken with on the phone but never met. I introduced myself and headed over to visit with my patient. He had been in and out of consciousness throughout the day. The daughter said he had not opened his eyes in several hours. As I approached him I quietly said, "Hey Yogi it's Boo Boo!" To our surprise he opened his eyes and looked at me. I smiled and then he reclosed his eyes. I visited with his daughter and we shared stories about her father. Within a half an hour his breathing began to change and he no longer opened his eyes. Shortly after that, he took his last breath and made his transition to the other side.

I stayed with the daughter, bringing her comfort and waited for the rest of the family to arrive. She turned to me and said, "Do you understand what just happened?" I was confused and didn't understand her statement. She then said, "I was exhausted and heading home when you arrived. If you hadn't come when you did, I would have left and missed my father's transition. You were sent here to keep me from leaving and I will forever be grateful to you!"

Tears welled up as I recalled the strong pulling to make that important visit which allowed her this moment in time. When we get something so strong pulling us to do something, listening and following that voice can allow for miraculous and magical things to unfold. Afterwards I sat outside looking up in to the most beautiful full moon I had ever seen and gave thanks for the wonderful opportunity that had been placed before me.

Songbird Sings

Songbird sings her song of love

Guided so gently from angels above

Her song found me so long ago

I felt her wings land effortlessly so

Our hearts did join, our wings did meet

Two birds in the night sharing beak to beak

We knew in our hearts, we both recognized

Our hearts knew each other and both
idolized

Each one aware . . . our wings always
together

Both kindred spirits, sharing one feather

It matters not what the body does show

We are Eternal spirits, always aglow

My songbird friend you touched my heart

And although miles away, not really apart

We know one another from across the pond

Our connection is forever, an eternal bond

Your wings touch my soul, my wings touches yours

We know we have met, many lifetimes before.

I'm with you now, right beside your nest

Wing touches wing, and you know the rest

I send you love, I reach out to you

My spirit will be there in all you do

I Met an Angel

I had a dream Sept, 11th, in the middle of the night. I had gone to see my patient Jan. She had the entire family there. The family was talking loudly and had loud music on. Jan could not hear me trying to talk with her. It appeared selfish on the part of the family in my opinion. Jan escorted me to another room where she had peace and quiet.

She crossed over the next day in the early afternoon. Her niece informed me that Jan had had a rough night. It was brought to my attention that the family of this patient may have been hovering around her and may have been stressing her. This would confirm the dream that I had. Perhaps we did encounter each other and perhaps she did have some peace in her spirit.

I met an Angel
And she gave me a smile
She asked could we visit
And talk for awhile
She shared her heart, her soul her glee
She touched deep down

The very depths of me
The joy was contagious
Her love so pure
I had just one wish
To find her a cure
Her life On Earth
Was nearing an end
Yet her courage remained
Over and over again
Her faith never faltered
Only Love did she show
No anger, no hatred
Just a bright, joyous glow
She's in my heart
For all Eternity
Remembered forever
She's my Angel you see

Brandi

My 9-year old patient, Brandi, had crossed over and I attended her wake. That evening I dreamed that she was lying there and opened her eyes. I ran to the family and others shouting, "She's not dead, she's not dead." I feel it was Brandi who came to me and reminded me she was still alive in spirit and that we truly don't die.

Brandi of Love
Brandi of Light
Each day you arise
And stand up and fight

Your strength is amazing
Your energy so free
Your soul already has
What I wish mine to be

Pure love full of hugs
No judgments at all
You get back on the horse
Every time that you fall

Each day there's a smile
And your eyes have a glow
A sparkle of light
Shining straight from your soul

If others could see
The real beauty of you
They just might be kinder
And get the real clue

We are here all as one
To love and to share
To help one another
And show them we care

You are my light
That keeps me glowing
I carry you with me
You help keep me going

I Love you

Nicholas

In the middle of the night I had Nicholas' dog Roxxie, come to me in a dream. She was trying to get my attention and I kept asking her how she found me, how did she know where I lived? She was happy to see me. The next morning I called and asked how Nicholas was. His wife informed me it was a rough night. He became agitated and she had to call a nurse to come over.

Roxxie was upset. The wife shooed her away and she hid in a closet. That was around the time she came to me in the dream. I shared this with the wife who exclaimed, "Oh, I bet she came to you in the middle of the night asking you for help as she knows you always helped Nick."

Cuddle Muffin

Brown wavy hair with eyelashes to match
A face that sparkles, a sunbeam to catch
Giggles galore, with googly sounds
Squeals of delight, when I dance around
The smile is contagious, your hugs so
strong
Your love shines bright, aw yes I belong
You look around with wonder and glee
You sing a song, directly for me
My heart you have won; my soul it glows
This river of love, somehow always flows
From you to me, from me to you
It's what love is so very true
You bring me a hug, a giggle, a smile
You let me love you, and hold you awhile
My heart is thus changed, forever you see
You bring me such joy; your love is so free
Each week I can't wait to see your smile
I walk into the door and get cuddled awhile

In honor of baby J* who has captured my
heart!

My Alzheimer's Patient

I was asked as a last resort to go and visit with an Alzheimer's patient in a memory care facility. She had been kicked out of other facilities for violent behavior. They wanted to try Massage Therapy and healing energy to see if it would help. The family and staff were so exhausted and felt they were running out of options.

At our first meeting the family, doctor, and staff were there. The patient was very combative and lashed out. I approached her and introduced myself by saying, "Hello, This is Pam, and I am here to give you a massage." Noteworthy was the fact that this patient had been the head nurse at a prominent hospital and had been getting regular massages her whole life.

She glared at me with anger and defiance and attempted to strike me. I moved to stand behind her and gently placed my hands on her shoulders. She was agitated for the first few minutes but then I felt her shoulders relax some and she became quiet.

The family and I decided at that time to try once a week massages. Her daughter was always present during these sessions. It was so fascinating to hear stories of how her mother ran a tight ship and oversaw all the other nurses. I knew deep down that she was in there somewhere, that she knew the massages were to help her. I vowed to somehow prove that.

The sessions continued over six months, most of the time she remained quiet and she never spoke. Afterwards, she would fall asleep and the staff and doctors were pleased at the progress. She began to lash out less and less. I always arrived at the same time and day each week with the exact same phrase, "Good morning, this is Pam and I am here to give you your massage."

Sometime around the six month mark, I arrived on time, getting ready to do my same routine. To my and the daughter's astonishment, when I said this is Pam and I am here . . . the patient stared at me and said the word "massage." Her daughter and I looked at each other and couldn't believe what we heard. This patient who never spoke a word, never acknowledged me or the touch, somehow deep within her, let me know that she was indeed in there somewhere and in this way was thanking me for the massage. It was a day that I will never forget and a reminder that what we do does make a difference, even if we don't realize it at the time. I never gave up and stayed committed to her and her healing.

Beautiful One

This beautiful child so full of grace
Who is this child who smiles up at me?

Sending forth rainbows right into my soul
Shooting beams of light deep into my heart

Making it bigger and wider than one can
imagine
I am the one sent to care for him, to bring
him comfort

Yet it seems he does the very same for me
Perhaps even more

He floods me with smiles
His eyes gleam with sunshine

He brightens my day with each visit
A love so pure, untainted

We share a Love of birds . . . Doves
They sing outside his window and soothe

A gift of love from another soul
Their song heals and brings peace

I am there for him, yet he is there for me
A little messenger, a ray of hope

Spreading love
Unconditional love

A reminder to me
That all are one

All are connected
That all we have to do to find love

Is to look within
It's already there

It is our legacy
It is who we are

Thank you my Beautiful One
I'm so glad God sent me

To sit with you awhile

Dedicated to Rodrigo, age 9

My Brother's Gift

Being a hospice Massage therapist, my focus is on the patient and alleviating their pain and bringing them comfort. I was aware of the family members and care-givers and interacted with them as well.

When my dear brother Taz came onto service in September of 2010, a whole new journey began for me as I was now a caregiver. My involvement with the whole process now became 24/7. What my brother blessed me with was giving me the gift of caring for him AND understanding the role a caregiver takes on, emotions and all.

I had always been thoughtful and caring of the caregivers but I now embrace them with a greater awareness of their pain, the grief, and their overwhelming stress. The morning I acknowledged this beautiful gift, I arrived at a patient's home and when the door opened I found a sobbing and over-whelmed spouse who needed some TLC. The patient could wait a few minutes. This spouse SO needed someone to listen and to just be there for them. My brother has recently ended his earthly journey and I have a newfound appreciation for all those caring for their loved ones. Thank you so much brother for this amazing gift.

Bird Song

She sits high up on the tree

Her freedom, her passion

Helps her to sing

To sing her passion

To share her freedom with the world

She sings at sunrise and sunset

Starting the day in gratitude

Ending the day being so thankful for the
song

The song that flows from her heart

The passion that flares forth from her soul

The places her wings carry her

Continues to amaze her and keeps her
going

Going from one destination to the next

Lingering only long enough to savor the joy

The excitement, that calls her to fly

To spread her wings in anticipation for the next adventure

She rarely sleeps, just long enough to rest her wings

She dreams of where the wind will take her next

She shudders in sheer ecstasy

Ever so ready, ever so willing

To trust the journey and the calling of her heart

The song that comes with each takeoff

She breathes in passion, and exhales pure love

And then she is off . . . with wild abandon

Where to now? Her heart can barely stand it!

And then she arrives

About the Author

Pam Sears has been a Licensed Massage Therapist and Bodyworker for more than 20 years. In addition she is an Infant Massage Instructor and Psychic Medium. This work has allowed her to follow her heart and practice in the healing field where she can share her passion and love for helping others. She has a private practice in Peoria, Arizona where she lives with her beloved boxer-pit rescue, Chelsea.

If you enjoyed this book you might also enjoy Pam's first book, *Whispers of the White Dove: Inspirational Poetry*.

To contact Pam visit her website at:
www.PamSears.com

Made in the USA
San Bernardino, CA
29 January 2018